A Durable Fire

New Poems

Books by May Sarton

A Durable Fire

New Poems
By MAY SARTON

NEW YORK

W · W · NORTON & COMPANY · INC ·

Some of these poems have appeared in the following journals:
*Contempora, Beloit Poetry Journal, The Lyric, Poetry,
Red Clay Reader, Pennsylvania Review, The Small Pond, Yankee.*

Library of Congress Cataloging in Publication Data

Sarton, May, 1912–
    A durable fire; new poems.

    I. Title.
PS3537.A832D8   811'.5'2   79-38404
ISBN 0-393-04362-2
ISBN 0-393-04375-4 (pbk)

1 2 3 4 5 6 7 8 9 0

FOR

Marynia F. Farnham

Contents

A Durable Fire

New Poems

"But Love is a durable fire,
    In the mind ever burning:
Never sick, never old, never dead,
    From itself never turning."

—SIR WALTER RALEIGH

1

For ten years I have been rooted in these hills,
The changing light on landlocked lakes,
For ten years have called a mountain, friend,
Have been nourished by plants, still waters,
Trees in their seasons,
Have fought in this quiet place
For my *self*.

I can tell you that first winter
I heard the trees groan.
I heard the fierce lament
As if they were on the rack under the wind.
I too have groaned here,
Wept the wild winter tears.
I can tell you that solitude
Is not all exaltation, inner space
Where the soul breathes and work can be done.
Solitude exposes the nerve,
Raises up ghosts.
The past, never at rest, flows through it.

Who wakes in a house alone
Wakes to moments of panic.
(Will the roof fall in?
Shall I die today?)
Who wakes in a house alone
Wakes to inertia sometimes,
To fits of weeping for no reason.
Solitude swells the inner space
Like a balloon.
We are wafted hither and thither
On the air currents.
How to land it?

I worked out anguish in a garden.
Without the flowers,

The shadow of trees on snow, their punctuation,
I might not have survived.

I came here to create a world
As strong, renewable, fertile,
As the world of nature all around me—
Learned to clear myself as I have cleared the pasture,
Learned to wait,
Learned that change is always in the making
(Inner and outer) if one can be patient,
Learned to trust myself.

2

The house is receptacle of a hundred currents.
Letters pour in,
Rumor of the human ocean, never at rest,
Never still. . . .
Sometimes it deafens and numbs me.

I did not come here for society
In these years
When every meeting is collision,
The impact huge,
The reverberations slow to die down.
Yet what I have done here
I have not done alone,
Inhabited by a rich past of lives,
Inhabited also by the great dead,
By music, poety—
Yeats, Valéry stalk through this house.
No day passes without a visitation—
Rilke, Mozart.
I am always a lover here,
Seized and shaken by love.

Lovers and friends,
I come to you starved
For all you have to give,
Nourished by the food of solitude,
A good instrument for all you have to tell me,

For all I have to tell you.
We talk of first and last things,
Listen to music together,
Climb the long hill to the cemetery
In autumn,
Take another road in spring
Toward newborn lambs.

No one comes to this house
Who is not changed.
I meet no one here who does not change me.

3

How rich and long the hours become,
How brief the years,
In this house of gathering,
This life about to enter its seventh decade.

I live like a baby
Who bursts into laughter
At a sunbeam on the wall,
Or like a very old woman
Entranced by the prick of stars
Through the leaves.

And now, as the fruit gathers
All the riches of summer
Into its compact world,
I feel richer than ever before,
And breathe a larger air.

I am not ready to die,
But I am learning to trust death
As I have trusted life.
I am moving
Toward a new freedom
Born of detachment,
And a sweeter grace—
Learning to let go.

I am not ready to die,
But as I approach sixty

I turn my face toward the sea.
I shall go where tides replace time,
Where my world will open to a far horizon
Over the floating, never-still flux and change.
I shall go with the changes,
I shall look far out over golden grasses
And blue waters. . . .

There are no farewells.

Praise God for His mercies,
For His austere demands,
For His light
And for His darkness.

Part One

"Set the table and sweep the floor—
Love will not come back to this door.

Plant your bulbs, sow summer flowers.
These be your joys, these your powers.

A cat for comfort, wood to burn,
And changing light as seasons turn.

Long hours alone and work to do—
These are your strength. These are for you."

So spoke myself. I listened well;
I thought that self had truth to tell.

But love came back after many a year,
Love all unasked knocked at the door,

Love all unasked broke down the door,
To bring me pain as it did before,

To bring me back lost poetry,
And all I'd meant alone to be.

What does myself now say to me?
"Open the door to Mystery.

Gather the grapes from any vine,
And make rich wine, and make rich wine.

Out of the passion comes the form,
And only passion keeps it warm.

Set the table, sweep the floor—
Forget the lies you told before."

Dear solid earth after ambiguous seas!
Oh gentle sand, incarnate mystery,
The body all at rest!

I battled waves, the depths of black and green,
Almost went down, heavy with death alone,
Now comforted and blest.

Goodbye to dangerous undertows, dispelled
For this calm wisdom never to be told
Where two souls melt.

We lie now all forgiven and enclosed
After the dispersed years when we supposed
All had been lost—and felt.

The nearly drowned, exhausted swimmer lies,
A shell in her clasped hand, salt in her eyes,
On this strange friendly shore.

It is enough simply to breathe again,
To breathe an easy long breath after pain,
Nor ask for more.

THE RETURN OF APHRODITE

Under the wave it is altogether still,
Alive and still, as nourishing as sleep,
Down below conflict, beyond need or will,
Where love flows on and yet is there to keep,
As unconstrained as waves that lift and break
And their bright foam neither to give nor take.

Listen to the long rising curve and stress,
Murmur of ocean that brings us the goddess.

From deep she rises, poised upon her shell.
Oh guiltless Aphrodite so long absent!
The green waves part. There is no sound at all
As she advances, tranquil and transparent,
To lay on mortal flesh her sacred mantle.

The wave recedes—she is drawn back again
Into the ocean where light leaves a stain.

INNER SPACE

We reach the area of no more hiding,
An inner space as open as the palm.
This is no ambience of childish confiding,
Exchange of lives, however great that charm.
Where we live now is far more exposed,
Not even to each other's need or gift,
But to the region love has proposed,
Open as a huge sky where planets lift,
Mysterious order, all shining and all clear—
No ambiguity to be refined
In a neurotic, dangerous atmosphere.
All is new here. We are to be defined.
We come together in an inner space
As rigorous, as deep as outer space.

A bluebird sudden as the flash of thought,
Embodied azure never to be caught.

The flowing white-on-white transparency
Of light through petals of a peony.

The shining ripple through tall meadow grass
Under the wind's invisible caress.

Unshadowed, vulnerable, smiling peace
Caught in one glance at a sleeping face.

Within love's new-sprung, light-shot, vivid green
My eyes are open. Angels can be seen.

They come and go as natural as you please—
What stirs? What wing there in the silent trees?

MOZART AGAIN

Now it is Mozart who comes back again
All garlanded in green.
Flute, harp, and trumpet, the sweet violin—
Each sound is seen.

Spring is a phrase, repeated green refrain,
Sound of new leaves springing.
I see the wind flowing like slanted rain,
Wind winging.

I learn this loving fresh, in ancient style
(Lightly time flows),
And mine a green world for pure joy awhile.
Listen, a rose!

Leaves are glissando. A long haunting phrase
Ripples the air—
This harpsichord of light that the wind plays.
Mozart is there.

MAY WALK

We stepped through light-and-shadow dapple
Stalking elusive intermittent song
Under fresh pink and green of flowering maple
And through white birch leaves newly sprung,
On to a spring snow fallen from the apple.

Redstart was first caught in our roving glasses,
And on we went, now warblering, now thrushing.
Is that an oven bird who flits and scratches?
Intent we scanned the woods for wings uprushing
From dank wet leaves and still watery grasses,

Till in the last hour of that walk in May
We caught a blue flash as you turned to go,
And radiant wings set their seal on the day.
What more could lovers ask than bluebird blue?
It felt like hope though you were on your way.

THE TREE PEONY

The old tree peony I had almost given up
Today presented a huge single flower.
Slowly, one by one, white petals,
Serrated, translucent,
Opened to the shaggy golden crown
At the heart.
My green world stood still
Around that presence,
Godlike, gathering the light.

How innocent the flesh that is born again
Like some awesome flower the Chinese sages
Devote a lifetime to contemplate and render,
Or I in my garden wait four years to see—
The pristine act of loving and being loved!

A CHINESE LANDSCAPE

I drove home through the morning, rich and still,
Where cloudy dragons floated every hill,
And winding rivers glittered and were lost
In the green haze of trees and rising mist,
The earth enfolded all around and blest
By autumn light, the fertile earth at rest.

As rich and gentled I after this harvest
Where every power fulfilled has come to rest,
And passionate love has learned a quiet ease
Like rivers winding through lyrical trees,
In time as spacious as early autumn light
When the mists rise and all is calm and bright.

For the first time I left you without woe,
So filled with wisdom I could even go
Holding our love at rest within my mind,
A Chinese painting where rich rivers wind
And lovers on a bridge over a small ravine
With their sole presence focus the huge scene.

THE GIFTED

From our joined selves long rivers start
We cannot find alone. The deepest sources
Well to the surface where we meet and part
To double all our singular resources.

My gifts are given and I leave you, gifted,
Filled with fresh powers and intimations.
So we are nourished; so, parting, we are lifted
Beyond the multitude of new sensations—

Transparent waters and soft shining sands,
Bermudas of the soul—but not for rest.
Love flows out from the rivers in our hands
Toward children, poems; each is doubly blest.

REEDS AND WATER

We look out, dazzled, at a shining lake
And up at light under long branches flowing
Along the silvery bark, a supple snake,
And leaves still dappled green before their going.

The background, ragged trees at water's edge,
But close at hand the pointed reeds define
And punctuate the glitter, a black wedge
That gives the casual scene a firm design.

Water and reeds—pure joy ran its course,
Compelling joy that drew us home, who now
Recapture the same light and feel its force
Flowing under the flesh as if a bough.

Reeds and still water—what better image spoken
For us, these autumn lovers, who must part
Over and over, the moment's shining broken,
Only to feel light flow back through the heart?

Over night it had emerged
From the contorted bisque shell
Of its cocoon
In a small cage
In the schoolroom.

We watched it,
Fragile furred antennae,
Wings still damp and wrinkled
Feeling their way
Toward this new incarnation,
And their slow, slow
Pulsation.

I stood there beside you
After another meeting,
Close to another parting,
And thought of our mothlike love—
The cocoons of separation,
The cramped hard times,
And wings pulsing slowly
After we come together.

How long has love to live
So close to hope,
So close to caged?
Now it is death again
In the cocoon
That limits and contorts.
The exquisite moth,
Its velvet softness,
Is a slow worm
Waiting and suffering
Toward huge quiet wings.

THE SNOW LIGHT

In the snow light,
In the swan light,
In the white-on-white light
Of a winter storm,
My delight and your delight
Kept each other warm.

The next afternoon—
And love gone so soon!—
I met myself alone
In a windless calm,
Silenced at the bone
After the white storm.

What more was to come?
Out from the cocoon,
In the silent room,
Pouring out white light,
Amaryllis bloom
Opened in the night.

The cool petals shone
Like some winter moon
Or shadow of a swan,
Echoing the light
After you were gone
Of our white-on-white.

WARNING

Now, in the brilliant sun,
In the winter cold,
Under this blazing sky,
We have had warning.
No one escapes. No one.
The brilliant young grow old.
The heart's frightening cry
Is heard at borning.
Accept, remember: all,
Even strong trees, die.
The whole world's burning.

Now in the brilliant day,
In the living blue,
Under this tent of Now,
We grasp hard truth,
Grasp it, not turn away—
You too, beloved, you.
Because today I know,
Don't speak to me of death,
But speak to me. Write often—
Your work, your joy, the snow.
Warm me with your breath.

SURFERS

Now we are balanced
On the high tide of the hour
Taking the wave with ease
As it breaks under us,
The tug and heave under our feet,
Flowing with, poised on
The dangerous power—
Experienced surfers who can ride it.

And then the landing,
To heave a heavy board
Onto hard wet sand,
The change of elements
We learn again at every parting
When we lie alone
And feel the long reverberation
Slowly dying down.

I have fought impermanence and change,
All my life tried to hold time still;
Now I must learn a new thing—
To take parting like a surfer,
Resume myself alone on the sand.
No rider now, a contemplative,
Permitting love its eloquent changes,
Glad to have ridden the big waves,
Glad to be very quiet now.

ALL DAY I WAS WITH TREES

Across wild country on solitary roads
Within a fugue of parting, I was consoled
By birches' sovereign whiteness in sad woods,
Dark glow of pines, a single elm's distinction—
I was consoled by trees.

In February we see the structure change—
Or the light change, and so the way we see it.
Tensile and delicate, the trees stand now
Against the early skies, the frail fresh blue,
In an attentive stillness.

Naked, the trees are singularly present,
Although their secret force is still locked in.
Who could believe that the new sap is rising
And soon we shall draw up amazing sweetness
From stark maples?

All day I was with trees, a fugue of parting,
All day lived in long cycles, not brief hours.
A tenderness of light before new falls of snow
Lay on the barren landscape like a promise.
Love nourished every vein.

A STORM OF ANGELS

Anarchic anger came to beat us down,
Until from all that battering we went numb
Like ravaged trees after a hurricane.
But in its wake we saw fierce angels come—
Not gentle and not kind—who threshed the grain
With their harsh wings, winnowed from waste.
They brought love to its knees in fearful pain.
Such angels come after the storm is past
As messengers of a true power denied.
They beat us down. For love, they thrash us free,
Down to the truth itself, stripped of our pride.
On those harsh wings they bring us agony.
Theirs is an act of grace, and it is given
To those in Hell who can imagine Heaven.

THE ANGELS AND THE FURIES

"Ange plein de gaîté connaissez-vous l'angoisse?"
—BAUDELAIRE

1

Have you not wounded yourself
And battered those you love
By sudden motions of evil,
Black rage in the blood
When the soul, *premier danseur,*
Spins toward a murderous fall?
The furies possess you.

2

Have you not surprised yourself
Sometimes by sudden motions
Or intimations of goodness,
When the soul, *premier danseur,*
Perfectly poised,
Could shower blessings
With a graceful turn of the head?
The angels are there.

3

The angels, the furies
Are never far away
While we dance, we dance,
Trying to keep a balance
To be perfectly human
(Not perfect, never perfect,
Never an end to growth and peril),
Able to bless and forgive
Ourselves.
This is what is asked of us.

4

It is light that matters,
The light of understanding.
Who has ever reached it
Who has not met the furies again and again?
Who has reached it without
Those sudden acts of grace?

To the country of silence
Welcome home, my love.
This is what we have to hold . . .

The leaves stitched by the wings of birds,
The skies inhabited by clouds
That lay their shadows on water and on distant hills,
The sudden shafts of light among the trees,
And the soft sifting fall of gold, for it is autumn,
Autumn again as the earth turns.

Welcome home, my soul,
To the country of silence
Where the soles of the feet are comforted
And the palms of the hands.

Forget the words.
They are torn raw out of another country,
The country where I live now
Trying to become myself without you.

They are torn harsh
Out of the country where you live,
Clawed at by human needs, boxed in time,
Till the whole being buzzes with this continuum
Of words, words as the only language.

Let us trust to silence;
It is healing.
And in that country where love is the genius
We make each other whole—
If only for a moment.
But it reverberates, that moment,
Its echoes are forever.

All that I know is that I leave you,
Always leave you in that white pain of loss,
Inhabited by poetry. . . .
Are hands wings that we feel them brush our eyelids
With such poignance?

What the child saw with dazzled eyes
And ran to meet
In a fury of exploration—
The radiant skies,
Blue over blue, blue over green,
Blue over white sand,
Changing light, clouds,
Shells, birds,
Sand under bare feet,
Sun on chilled skin,
And the plunge into lucid green
Beyond the broken wave
Dragging its treasure . . .

What the child plundered
With eyes, mouth, hands,
We bring home now
With a handful of shells
To sort and think over.
What can we discard
From an island week?
What can we keep?
What happened there?

All that we shared
Must be free to roam,
Not held too close,
Given to the singular mind
To explore alone
In that deep place
Where the sensuous image
Marries the soul.

Now it is the intermittent descent
Of roseate wings
As, one by one,
The spoonbills float down—

At sunset, rose against rose—
To rest on still water.

Now the sudden vision,
Explosive,
Of the sharp red crest,
The staccato hammer
Of the pileated woodpecker.

Now the solitary hawk at dusk,
His great presence
Ominous, intense,
Watching.

Now the flittering, darting
Of shore birds in and out of the foam,
The sharp practical eyes,
The swift, skittering legs.

This is an Easter
Of the intensely visual
Translated to the inmost being,
Where we shall learn (perhaps)
To float the mind as if on wings,
Supported by currents of memory
Above the thickets of all that stops the flow
Between us,
Our disparate lives.

Apart, we meet on these calm memories,
Among essences and absolutes—
Long draughts of sky,
Attentive looks
At the detail of bill, webbed foot,
Or small black line
Above a warbler's eye.
An Easter strangely bare
Of our human sorrow,
Complexity, irritations;
Love this time
Wind-threshed, wave-beaten
To impersonal joy.

After the fervor,
This new detachment.
Hold them in balance
And we come to the wisdom
That says "forever,"
To the Easter of human love,
Or, if you will, an island.

FULFILLMENT

We hold it in our keeping, even apart,
Twin trees whose pollen has been swiftly crossed,
And all this sumptuous flowering of the heart
Will grow rich fruit, nor anything be lost.

Fall, petals, fall, cover the green with snow!
There is no grieving loss, and no alarm.
The palaces of leaves begin to show
The small fruit swelling in the summer calm.

So grave a state of being holds us still
There at the center where the roots drink deep.
The leaves may tremble but the winds fulfill
The autumn fruit, knotting when flowers sleep.

There is no place for yearning, we must grow.
We live now in the heart of Mystery,
Part of Creation's deepest urge and flow
To which bears witness every flower and tree.

Part Two

The Autumn Sonnets

1

Under the leaves an infant love lies dead,
But we will have no mourning. It is good.
This was the useless crying in my head.
This was the grieving fury in my blood.
The house is being buried—so it seems—
Under the brittle trash of leaves let go,
The infant anguish and the infant dreams,
Soon to be lost forever under snow,
While sleeping beauty sleeps toward a spring
When Love, the prince, will come back through the green
As once he did when time was on the wing,
And he will push aside a flowery screen
To wake a woman, full-grown, rich in light,
Whose infant cries were stilled one autumn night.

2

If I can let you go as trees let go
Their leaves, so casually, one by one;
If I can come to know what they do know,
That fall is the release, the consummation,
Then fear of time and the uncertain fruit
Would not distemper the great lucid skies
This strangest autumn, mellow and acute.
If I can take the dark with open eyes
And call it seasonal, not harsh or strange
(For love itself may need a time of sleep),
And, treelike, stand unmoved before the change,
Lose what I lose to keep what I can keep,
The strong root still alive under the snow,
Love will endure—if I can let you go.

3

I wake to gentle mist over the meadow,
The chilling atmosphere before sunrise
Where half my world lies still asleep in shadow
And half is touched awake as if by eyes.

Sparse yellow leaves high in the air are struck
To sudden flame as the first rays break through
And all the brightness gathers to that mark,
While floating in the dim light far below
A monarch settles on an autumn crocus
For one last drink before impending flight.
The slow pulse of the wings brings into focus
The autumn scene and all its dark and bright,
And suddenly the granite rock is split
As sun lights up exactly half of it.

4

I never thought that it could be, not once,
The Muse appearing in warm human guise,
She the mad creature of unhappy chance
Who looked at me with cold Medusa eyes,
Giver of anguish and so little good.
For how could I have dreamed that you would come
To help me tame the wildness in my blood,
To bring the struggling poet safely home?
The grand design is clear, but we must work
To make it viable. The vision presses,
And I have never doubted its true mark
Where all I suffer stems from all that blesses;
For what I know, both vulnerable and great,
Is Love, that prince, who teaches me to wait.

5

After a night of rain the brilliant screen
Below my terraced garden falls away.
And there, far off, I see the hills again
On this, a raw and windy, somber day.
Moment of loss, and it is overwhelming
(Crimson and gold gone, that rich tapestry),
But a new vision, quiet and soul-calming,
Distance, design, are given back to me.
This is good poverty, now love is lean,
More honest, harder than it ever was
When all was glamoured by a golden screen.

] 44 [

The hills are back, and silver on the grass,
As I look without passion or despair
Out on a larger landscape, grand and bare.

6

As if the house were dying or already dead;
As if nobody cared—and, in fact, who does?
(Whose feet but mine wear out the painted tread?
Who listens for the fly's autumnal buzz?
Who climbs the stair to a wide upstairs bed?);
As if the house were prepared every day
By an odd owner with madness in her head
For visitors who never come to stay,
For love that has no time here or elsewhere,
Who keeps fresh flowers on each mantel still,
And sweeps the hearth and warms the chilling air
As if to keep the house alive on will—
Truth is, her daily battle is with death,
Back to the wall and fighting for each breath.

7

Twice I have set my heart upon a sharing,
Twice have imagined a real human home,
Having forgotten how some fiercer caring
Demands this naked solitude for loam.
Now love pours out in light from every wound
I know the kind of home this cannot be,
And know more savagely what I have found—
An open door into great mystery.
I came here first for haven from despair
And found a deeper root than passionate love,
A wilder inscape and a safer lair
Where the intrinsic being kept alive.
Home is a granite rock and two sparse trees
As light and shadow may inhabit these.

8

I ponder it again and know for sure
My life has asked not love but poetry,
Asked less for joy than power to endure.

More than ten years this house has sheltered me.
The challenge never changed. It always was
What I could make out of sheer deprivation,
The falling leaf, the silver on the grass,
Sometimes a piercing moment of sensation
As when I look out into autumn haze
And catch under the apple a young buck
To meet his long attentive fearless gaze.
The rest has been work and a little luck,
Keeping the balance between loneliness
And the dark heart of silence that can bless.

9

This was our testing year after the first
When we were drunk on love and drunk on light.
Unquenchable our hunger and our thirst
For shining presence through the longest night.
Somehow we wrote each other every day,
Mingled disparate lives in rich exchange.
All must be now. What if it did not stay?
All must be tightly held for fear of change.
But such fierce ardor soon wore itself out.
The phone became a monstrous instrument,
And words tangled themselves into a knot.
Something got frayed of all we felt and meant.
It was the year of testing. Now we know
Exactly what was asked: we had to grow.

10

We watched the waterfalls, rich and baroque,
As a bright stream flowed into an impasse
And there exploded over jagged rock
In shining sheaves as if of liquid glass.
Within the roar no spoken word could fall.
We were enclosed by water, rock, and tree,
And carried far outside the personal
To rest on primal force and symmetry.
Across turbulent water and still air
A gold leaf floated slowly past.

Our eyes, open to all that we can share,
Gave us the luminous design at rest.
We stood together in its clarity,
Because, being together, we could see.

11

For steadfast flame wood must be seasoned,
And if love can be trusted to last out,
Then it must first be disciplined and reasoned
To take all weathers, absences, and doubt.
No resinous pine for this, but the hard oak
Slow to catch fire, would see us through a year.
We learned to temper words before we spoke,
To force the furies back, learned to forbear,
In silence to wait out erratic storm,
And bury tumult when we were apart.
The fires were banked to keep a winter warm
With heart of oak instead of resinous heart,
And in this testing year beyond desire
Began to move toward durable fire.

Part Three

FEBRUARY DAYS

Who could tire of the long shadows,
The long shadows of the trees on snow?
Sometimes I stand at the kitchen window
For a timeless time in a long daze
Before these reflected perpendiculars,
Noting how the light has changed,
How tender it is now in February
When the shadows are blue not black.

The crimson cyclamen has opened wide,
A bower of petals drunk on the light,
And in the snow-bright ordered house
I am drowsy as a turtle in winter,
Living on light and shadow
And their changes.

NOTE TO A PHOTOGRAPHER

For some months now I have lived
With that pale blue eye of spring—
A pond deep in a brown world,
Bare ground, lines of young fruit trees
Not yet in leaf.
Shining like a fish scale
In the earthy world
It gathers all the light there is.

Your pocket of sky, Photographer,
Has accompanied the winter mood,
A discreet promise
Where my anxious eye
Comes to rest on hope.

Here in New England where the ice still grips
And pussy willows have not put on fur,
The masts are earthbound of the sleeping ships,
And only clammers on the beaches stir.
All seems exhausted by its own withholding,
Its own withstanding. There is no unfolding.
Even the new moon promises no better
Than a thin joke about much colder weather.

This harsh world locks itself up in the season.
It is clearly not the time and not the place
To ask for summer love, for more than reason,
To hope to lift the cloud from any face.
Look at the trees, how even they determine
To hold their leaves back under the tough skin.
"Keep snug" is their advice, and they endure,
For frost is on the way again for sure.

Yet in New England before spring I've seen
The sea unfold as sumptuous as silk,
Have watched the cold world tilt back into green,
And watched the waves spill out like foaming milk—
Till the eye, starved for color and for light,
Wept at such majesty beside such blight,
Would rush to break trees open, and to bring
To this locked world torrents of English spring!

A rich profusion of familiar flowers,
All sunflecked, checquered, alive to the wind;
A gentle explosion of light in bosks and bowers,
So natural it seemed but half designed;
The arbor, an ardor of roses and clematis,
The borders, a passion of stained-glass blue and white
With spires of lupin and foxglove, lilies and iris,
All troubled and shining between shadow and light—

Chaotic splendor framed by a clipped lawn
Spread out under a cluster of apple trees
Where empty chairs and table stand forlorn,
Emblems of all our summers and all our teas.
Here Franz the goose, a cock, a guinea hen,
Two ducks, a Persian cat, all begged for a crumb,
And every bird and beast took part in the scene.
Here we learned the joys of the peaceable kingdom.

I see it now, an illuminated page.
The assiduous monk in his joy did not spare
Costly vermilion and gold, nor the rich sage.
He painted a garden haunting as a prayer
Where children rest still in long revery.
Stay, precious light on the snow-white peony!

COMPOSITION

Here is the pond, here sky, and the long grasses
That lean over the water, a slow ripple
Under the slightest wandering air that passes
To shift the scene, translating flat to stipple
On still blue water and troubling the green masses.

Three elements are spaced and subtly joined
To rest the restless mind and lift us where
Nothing in us is baffled or constrained,
Who wake and sleep as casual as they are,
And contain earth, and water, and the wind.

Take blue; take green; take the pale gold sand;
Take the slow changing shimmer of the air;
Take a huge sky above a steadfast land;
Take love, the tiger ocean in its lair,
And gentle it like grass under the wind.

AUTUMN AGAIN

It is an open world and we are naked,
Given the delicate newborn light,
Pale autumn skies, and all things clear,
Airy, in some ways insubstantial.
Petal and leaf gone, pulp yields to pith,
The diffuse mass to nerve and structure.
Now early sunsets linger on and on
In bands of yellow over darkened hills—
Hills that were canceled out in summer.

We are the creatures of seasonal change—
Chipmunks, slim and golden, run about
Hoarding against the snow, and absent jays
Come flocking out of the woods for seed.
Raccoons grow plump. What shall I keep
Of all the summer's prodigal green gifts?
The fat brown seeds of love-in-a-mist?
Round rose haws rich in nourishment?
A cord of wood stacked on the porch for luck?
A ream of yellow paper for the harvest?
It is an open world!

WINTER CAROL

Black mood, away!
For all that's marred
And was ill-starred,
It's a new day.
Here comes the jay!

Dagger for beak,
And crest pure pride,
Bold and black-eyed,
His voice a shriek,
He shames the weak.

He takes the day,
The cruel ice,
As cats take mice
In pouncing play.
Black mood, away!

Be gone, sad woe!
For all that's marred
And was ill-starred,
The bright blue bravo
Flies in, flies low.

Part Four

BURIAL

The old man who had dug the small pit
Opened the two boxes with a penknife
And let the ashes fall down into it,
The ashes of this husband and his wife,
My father and my mother gently laid
Into the earth and mingled there for good.

We watched the wind breathe up an ashen breath
And blow thin smoke along the grass—
And that was all: the bitterness of death
Lifted to air, laid in the earth. All was
Terribly silent where four people stood
Tall in the air, believing what they could.

OF GRIEF

You thought it heartless
When my father fell down
Dead in his splendid prime,
Strong as a green oak thrown,
That all I did was praise
Death for this kindness,
Sang with a voice unbroken
Of the dear scholar's days,
His passion of a lifetime—
And my loss never spoken.

Judge of another's grief?
Weigh out that grief in tears?
I did not weep my father,
The rich, the fulfilled years.
What slow death have you known?
When no hope or belief
Can help, no loving care?
We watch and weep alone.
My heart broke for my mother.
I buried grief with her.

It is the incomplete,
The unfulfilled, the torn
That haunts our nights and days
And keeps us hunger-born.
Grief spills from our eyes,
Unwelcome, indiscreet,
As if sprung from a fault
As rivers seam a rock
And break through under shock.
We are shaken by guilt.

There are some griefs so loud
They could bring down the sky,
And there are griefs so still
None knows how deep they lie,
Endured, never expended.

There are old griefs so proud
They never speak a word;
They never can be mended.
And these nourish the will
And keep it iron-hard.

PRISONER AT A DESK

It is not so much trying to keep alive
As trying to keep from blowing apart
From inner explosions every day.
I sit here, open to psychic changes,
Living myself as if I were a land,
Or mountain weather, the quick cycles
Where we are tossed from the ice age
To bursts of spring, to sudden torrents
Of rain like tears breaking through iron.
It is all I can do to keep tethered down.

No prisoner at a desk, but an ocean
Or forest where waves and gentle leaves
And strange wild beasts under the groves
And whales in all their beauty under the blue
Can gently rove together, still untamed,
Where all opens and breathes and can grow.

Whatever I have learned of good behavior
Withers before these primal powers.
Here at the center governess or censor
No longer has command. The soul is here,
Inviolable splendor that exists alone.

Prisoner at a desk? No, universe of feeling
Where everything is seen, and nothing mine
To plead with or possess, only partake of,
As if at times I could put out a hand
And touch the lion head, the unicorn.
Here there is nothing, no one, not a sound
Except the distant rumor, the huge cloud
Of archetypal images that feed me . . .

Look, there are finches at the feeder.
My parrot screams with fear at a cloud.
Hyacinths are budding. Light is longer.

BIRTHDAY PRESENT

Renewal cannot be picked
Like a daffodil
In a swift gesture,
Cannot be cut like a pussy willow
And brought into the house.
It cannot even be imagined
Like the blue sky
We have not seen for days.

But we can be helped toward it.
True love gave me time,
Gave me, for myself alone,
This whole open day
We would have spent together.

True love gave me this—
Harder to find
Than a hummingbird's nest,
Rare as the elusive
Scent of arbutus
Under sodden leaves,
More welcome than a cup
Of spring water
After long drought.

I hold it in my hands,
I breathe it in,
I drink it,
While fifty-nine years
Of ardor and tenderness,
Of struggle and creation—
The whole complex bundle—
Falls away in a streak of light
Like a shooting star,
As the soul,
Unencumbered,
Alive, ageless,
Meets the pristine moment:
Poetry again.

ELEGY
(for Louise Bogan)

The death of this poet hurts us terribly,
As if a planet sank down through the sky.

Just so she was remote, just so she shone.
Singular light has gone now she is gone.

Where are they now, the aqueous green eyes,
Her violent heart, her innocent surprise?

How shall we live without her ironies
That kept her crystal clear and made us wise?

Louise, Louise, why did you have to go
In this hard time of wind and shrouding snow,

When even trees are strange and much too still,
And absence on us like some psychic chill?

We cannot have you back, but you are there,
A shining presence on our ghostly air,

Wherever soul meets soul on this dark plain
And we are worth your clarifying pain.

Deprived, distraught, often despairing,
You kneaded a celestial bread for sharing.

I have not wept a tear, nor shall I do,
Stripped to this naked praise that shines for you.

February 10, 1970

Part Five

Letters to
a Psychiatrist

CHRISTMAS LETTER, 1970

1

These bulbs forgotten in a cellar,
Pushing up through the dark their wan white shoots,
Trying to live—their hopeless hope
Has been with me like an illness
For twenty years or more,
The image of what tries to be born
But dies for lack of light.

Today I saw it again in the stare
Of the homeless cat, that hunger
Not for food only, but to be taken in,
And to trust enough to risk it . . .
Shelter, life itself. Can I tame her?
Come the worst cold, will she freeze?

How marvelous to know you can save,
Restore, nourish the abandoned,
That the lifeline is there
In your wise hands, Marynia!

2

"Yes," you say, "of course at Christmas
Half the world is suicidal."
And you are there. You answer the phone—
The wry voice with laughter in it.
Again and again the lifeline is thrown out.
There is no end to the work of salvage
In the drowning high seas of Christmas
When loneliness, in the name of Christ
(That longing!), attacks the world.

3

One by one, they come from their wilderness
Like shy wild animals
Weeping blood from their wounds,

Wounds they dare not look at
And cannot bind or heal alone.

What is it that happens then
In the small closed room
Where someone listens,
Where someone answers,
Where someone cares,
Whom they cannot hurt
With their sharp infant teeth,
With their sharp old antlers?

What does she do,
This doctor, this angel,
Who holds so many
In her human hands?
How does she heal the animal pain
So the soul may live?

4

No Ceres, she, no Aphrodite;
She cannot provide the harvest
Nor the longed-for love.

This angel must be anarchic,
Fierce, full of laughter,
Will neither punish
Nor give absolution,
Is always acute, sometimes harsh.
Still the impersonal wing
Does shelter, provides a place, a climate
Where the soul can meet itself at last.

There is no way out,
Only the way deeper and deeper inward.
There are no solutions,
But every word is action,
As is every silence.
On a good day the patient
Has used his reason
To cut through secret evasions,

Secret fears,
Has experienced himself
As a complex whole.

But angels do not operate
By any means we can define.
They come when they are needed.
(I can tell you of the resonance,
The beat of wings
Threshing out truth
Long after the hour is past.)
When they have gone
The light-riddled spirit
Is as alone as ever,
But able to fly its course again
Through the most hostile sky.

5

I know what it is like, Marynia.
Once I watched a jay flopping, helpless,
In the snow outside this window—
I brought it in, managed to pull out the quill
Shot through just under the eye.
I know what it is to have to be brutal
Toward the badly crippled
In order to set them free.
Then it was Easter and I saw the jay
Fly off whole into the resurrected air.

Now it is Christmas
When infant love, vulnerable beyond our knowing,
Is born again to save the world.

And for whatever crucifixions it will suffer,
Angel, be blessed for your wings.

THE FEAR OF ANGELS

It is not what they intend,
But we are light-struck,
Blinded by their presence,
When all they want is to *see* us.

We have to turn away,
Cannot look at the huge, deep Unknown
That speaks through their eyes.
They strip us down to the infant gaze
Still deep in the sky,
Still rooted somewhere we cannot remember.

Angel, look away.
I cannot afford to yield the last defence,
To go back—

"Not back, but deeper,"
Said the angel, folding his wings
To wait.

1

After the whirlwind when all things
Were blown out of their courses
In the fiery gust,
After the whirlwind when all beams were crossed
And passionate love confused,
Its clear path lost,
Where nothing fused,
But all was burned and forced,
The psyche nearly cracked
Under the blast,
After the earthquake passed

How did it happen
That cool eyes looked out
On darkness and the storm
And cut the ties
That meant chaos and harm
So that true mysteries
Might act and charm
The haunted spirit back
To its own realm?

What did the angel do
To make all levels straight
Within that sheaf
Of troubled sense and fear,
Set every beam on its own path
At last untangled,
Singular and bright,
So that nothing was lost,
No slightest hope
Was blurred by childish grief
Outside its scope,
But all was still and clear,
So still and bright
No galaxy of stars
Could shine more absolute
On winter night?

2

I watched the psychic surgeon,
Stern, skilled, adroit,
Cut deep into the heart
And yet not hurt.
I watched it happen—
Old failures, old obsessions
Cut away
So blood could flow
A clear course through
Choked arteries again.
There was no pain.
My eyes, wide open,
Watched every move
In absolute surrender
To superior power.
I saw it happen
In one luminous hour
(No anesthetic given),
An act of extreme grace
And sovereign love.
From Hell I entered Heaven
And bowed my head,
Where nothing had been suffered,
But all given.

3

Simple acceptance
Of things as they are;
Finished, that strained arc,
Leap of the salmon upstream
Climbing waterfalls,
Sublimation
Of one death or another,
The cruel ascension
Toward loss.

Now things as they are—
Spring of the fern as it uncoils,
Brute rock broken
To show the crystal,
Light-shot February skies—

All, all have been given
After the whirlwind.

This is no repetition
Of unresolved attachments
And deprivations,
No turn of the old wheel.
It is altogether new.

4

In the terrifying whirlwind
When the mother is resurrected
(How many times, angelic doctor,
How many times?)
Every defence against grief goes.
There is no future,
Only excruciating repetition
Of the unburied past.
For the last time
I was torn to pieces
By my mother's anguish,
Unattainable goddess
Whose compassionate eyes
Understood me so well—
And took my heart.

I do not have to love you
As I loved her,
To be devastated, but,
Angel and surgeon of the psyche,
I am free to love you now
Outside all the myths,
The confused dreams,
Beyond all the barriers,
In the warm natural light
Of simple day.
I am allowed to give you
Unstrained, flowing,
Wise-infant
To wise-mother love.

You broke the spell;
You with your whippets around you

Like some lady in a tapestry
Said to the unicorn,
"If the child needs the mother,
The mother needs the child."
So be it.

5

In middle age we starve
For ascension,
Look back to childhood teachers
But have outgrown them.
Mature love needs new channels.
How long has it been—
What starving years—
Since I was permitted
To cherish wisdom?

I bend tenderly
Toward the young
With open heart and hands.
I share in a great love
With my equal.
Every day I learn better
About how to give
And how to receive love.
But there is still the need
To be filial toward someone,
To be devoted,
Humble and enlightened.
I need to remain teachable
For one who can teach me.
With you all green things flourish,
All flowers may be freely given,
All fears can be expressed,
No childish need is sneered at,
No adult gift unrecognized.

Speak to me
Of the communion of saints
On earth.

6

Light cannot be described,
Is nothing in itself,

Transforms all it touches.
The flower becomes transparent flame.
A plain white wall
Is marbled by flowing water,
And in the soul's realm
Light defines feeling,
Makes distinctions.

In the light
Of this penetrating mind,
Vivid response,
Total awareness,
I find myself
In a new landscape—
Fra Angelico's Paradise
(It was dear to my mother
I suddenly remember)
Where souls, released at last,
Dance together
On the simple grass.

Look, there is an owl in the tree;
A fling of lambs in February snow.
There is a donkey waving her long ears.
There is a child
With flowers in her hands.

There is a continuum
(Those garlands of joined dancers)
Of redemptive love.

I'll keep it
For a million years.

I SPEAK OF CHANGE

Tumult as deep and formal as in dance
Seizes me now for every scheduled hour.
I meet you at the marrow of your power,
The Hindu *darshan*, action by pure presence.
The room is filled with words, but what I hear
Is silence growing gently like a plant
And that real space around us what I want,
The space where subtle change is drawing near.
I speak of influence as a navigator
Reckons upon the influence of a star—
Now, for a time, the light is where you are.
As the earth turns, it will be darker later.
I speak of change that cannot yet be spoken
As of a circle that will gently close
(When time and distance break the bond between us)
And will complete itself as it is broken,
So rich and rounded these ultimate hours
Where being more than love between us flowers.

EASTER 1971

I, in my winter poverty, alone,
Celebrate riches, come to this Easter
Humbler than I have ever been,
Closer to all that answers solitude—
The light, birds' wings, perfect silence
Of windless star-illuminated nights,
Even a sudden April storm of snow.

"Preposterous" you say about the road agent
Who has not ploughed you out this time,
And then your vivid anger turns to laughter.
Preposterous your power to enhance and probe
Whatever life may bring, your mixture
Of fervor and detachment, those antiphonies
Where the soul of a poet feeds and rests.

Preposterous your power to harmonize
And bring to its fruition the poet's gift,
Always dependent on some human eye,
On one who *sees* (never mind feeling).

Alone, without hope of being otherwise,
I come to this Easter newly rich and free
In all my gifts. I do not need your eyes
To know that we are close to an epiphany.

Fervor, detachment meet as life meets art.
There will be no tangible loss when we part,
For this epiphany is flowering from acceptance
Of a structured, impersonal, and holy dance.

THE CONTEMPLATION OF WISDOM

To contemplate this human wisdom,
To contemplate this presence as it acts,
Slowly unraveling the mystery of pain,
Has been a task both joyful and severe.

Partaking wisdom, I have been given
The sum of many difficult acts of grace,
A vital fervor disciplined to patience.
This cup holds grief and balm in equal measure,
Light, darkness. Who drinks from it must change.

Wisdom can only give when someone takes.
To take you I go deeper into darkness
Than I could dare until this crucial year.
To take you I must take myself to judgment,
Accepting what can never be fulfilled—
My life, at best, poised on a knife-edge
Between what art would ask and what life takes;
Yet I am lavish with riches made from loss.
I summon up fresh courage from your courage.

Before we part, give me your love.
I'll use it as the key to solitude.